Scholastic Canada Biographies

CANADIAN LEADERS

Maxine Trottier

illustrated by

Alan & Lea Daniel

Scholastic Canada Ltd.
Toronto New York London Auckland Sydney
Mexico City New Delhi Hong Kong Buenos Aires

To the memory of my sister-in-law, Ruth Doig,
a leader in education

– M.T.

Photo Credits

Page 6: W. Décary, engraved by J. Armstrong, *Ville-Marie en 1642*, National Archives of Canada C-007885
Page 10 (upper): P.L. Morin, *Montréal vu à vol d'oiseau de 1645 à 1650*, National Archives of Canada C-006031; (lower) Courtesy of Peter Warren, Director, History of Medicine program, University of Manitoba
Page 11: Courtesy of M. Camille Boily, Monere Public Art
Page 17: From a drawing by Lieutenant Pilkington copied by Mrs. Simcoe, *The Mohawk Village, Grand River, 1793*, National Archives of Canada C-084448
Page 18 (left): Courtesy of Her Majesty's Chapel of the Mohawks; (right) Courtesy of the Museums of Burlington, Joseph Brant Museum Collection, Burlington, Ontario
Page 19: Courtesy of the City of Brantford
Page 23: National Archives of Canada C-000733
Page 26: Prof. Oliver Buell, C.W. Spencer Fonds, Canadian Railroad Historical Association Archives 82.26.1.23
Page 28: National Archives of Canada C-006536
Page 29 (upper): William Notman, *Sir John A. Macdonald, K.C.B.*, National Archives of Canada C-030440; (lower) William James Topley, *Old Guard Dinner*, National Archives of Canada PA-009068
Page 33: Courtesy of the Royal Canadian Mounted Police
Page 34: Glenbow Archives NA-294-1
Page 35: Glenbow Archives NA-2382-3
Page 38, 41 (left and lower), 45: CP Archives; CP/Blaise Edwards; CP/Peter Bregg; CP/Doug Ball
Page 41 (right), 42, 44: National Archives of Canada PA-111213; National Archives of Canada PA-110806; National Archives of Canada PA-141503
Page 43 (left and right): Sun Media Corp.

National Library of Canada Cataloguing in Publication

Trottier, Maxine
Canadian leaders / Maxine Trottier ; illustrations by Alan and Lea Daniel.

(Scholastic Canada biographies)
ISBN 0-439-96104-1

1. Canada—Biography—Juvenile literature. I. Daniel, Alan, 1939- II. Daniel, Lea III. Title. IV. Series.

FC25.T765 2004   j971'.009'9   C2004-900881-1

6 5 4 3 2 1   Printed in Canada   04 05 06 07 08

Contents

Jeanne Mance
The Angel of the Colony

Jeanne Mance's comfortable life began in Langres, France, on November 12, 1606. Her father was a state official – a magistrate. When Jeanne was 20 years old, her mother died and she had to share in the upbringing of some of her 11 brothers and sisters. During the Thirty Years War in France, she volunteered as a nurse for the wounded and those ill from the plague. This helped to prepare her for what lay ahead.

In 1640 Jeanne heard from her cousin Nicolas about New France, far across the Atlantic, and how missionary priests were working to convert the

Native peoples to the Catholic faith. Deeply moved, she travelled to Paris to learn more and, once there, met many wealthy people. One of them, Madame Angélique de Bullion, asked her to found a hospital for a new colony that was being planned. Jeanne agreed to this perilous mission – and a contract was drawn up. Madame de Bullion gave Jeanne about 40,500 *livres*, promising more money once she was settled in New France.

On May 9, 1641, two ships set sail from the port of La Rochelle, France, with a party of 41 men and 4 women. On one of the ships was the expedition's leader, Paul de Chomedey, Sieur de Maisonneuve. Jeanne Mance was on the other.

Although they left together, the two ships separated. Jeanne's ship experienced good weather and arrived at the town of Quebec on August 8. Maisonneuve's vessel — the *Sainte-Jeanne*, which had been named after Jeanne — was caught in violent storms and had to turn back three times. It didn't reach Quebec until September 20.

Winter set in and the St. Lawrence River froze. Not until May 8, 1642, once the ice had melted, did Jeanne's party set out again to establish their new colony. They made their way up the river in a pinnace (a flat-bottomed sailing boat), two rowboats and a barge. There were about 40 people — Maisonneuve, a priest, soldiers, and three married couples who had their children with them. On May 17 they arrived at an island. This would become Ville-Marie, the settlement that would later be called Montreal.

Tents were put up to serve as the first shelters. With help, Jeanne decorated an altar on which the

Ville-Marie in 1642

first Catholic Mass was said. As night fell, it was lit with fireflies caught in the meadow.

That summer a palisade was built for protection. All around lay the wilderness, which Jeanne found to be beautiful. She said, "Along the banks of the river . . . one could see only meadows enamelled with flowers in every colour of a charming beauty."

More ships carrying 12 new settlers and supplies for the town of Ville-Marie arrived in August. In the fall of 1642, Jeanne's hospital — which they called Hôtel-Dieu — was founded. That December the waters of the St. Lawrence River began to rise, but the settlement was spared. To give thanks, Maisonneuve ordered a cross to be built. He carried it up the hill and set it in the ground. To this day a cross still stands at the top of Mount Royal in Montreal.

By the next summer, the Iroquois began to attack the fort. Jeanne cared tirelessly for the wounded colonists. The records of the priests state that she nursed an Algonquin chief named Pachirini back to health. He was later baptized and given the name Charles.

The construction of a proper Hôtel-Dieu was completed in 1645. It was a simple wooden building that measured about 18 by 7 metres, surrounded by a trench and a stockade. There were six beds for men and two for women. Jeanne had a chamber for herself.

The Hurons became allies of the colony, but the Iroquois did not want the settlers on their land and the attacks continued. With the help of a servant, during this dangerous time, Jeanne prepared medicines and nursed the sick and wounded. Over the years she and her companions endured harsh winters so cold that the drinking water froze within 15 minutes. The simple houses were full of holes and cracks. On many mornings snow had to be swept from the rooms.

In 1650 Jeanne Mance sailed to France to plead
for more money for the colony. She was successful,
but when she returned the next year she had to close
the hospital because of the Iroquois attacks. With
the other settlers, she took refuge in the fort.

Maisonneuve decided to journey to France to
get help. If he failed, they would have to abandon
the settlement. Jeanne Mance refused to give up.
She made a decision, one that saved Montreal. She
gave him the 22,000 *livres* she had brought back for
the hospital. He sailed to France and was back two
years later with 120 soldiers who defended the town
for the next five years.

With the soldiers were some women and
children. One woman, Marguerite Bourgeoys, had
come with the idea of starting a school. She and
Jeanne became close friends.

Early Montreal (Ville-Marie), showing (A) the Fort; (B) Hôtel-Dieu;
(C) Maisonneuve's residence, built in 1652

In 1658 Jeanne and Marguerite made a return voyage to France. Jeanne brought back three Sisters of St. Joseph to help in the hospital. It was a difficult 67-day voyage and typhus broke out on the ship. Once back in Montreal, Jeanne began to live a quieter life as her health slowly failed.

The present Hôtel-Dieu, Montreal, Quebec, built in 1861

Jeanne Mance died in Montreal on June 18, 1673, her friend Marguerite at her side. She was buried in the chapel of Hôtel-Dieu two days later. With her skill and leadership, Montreal had grown from its original 40 people to 1400 settlers.

Today her statue stands in front of Hôtel-Dieu in Montreal, and the park at the foot of Mount Royal is named for her. Jeanne Mance was Canada's first lay nurse, and the award named after her is our country's highest nursing honour. "The Angel of the Colony," she will always be remembered for her bravery and devotion to New France.

Statue of Jeanne Mance in Montreal, Quebec

Joseph Brant
A Mohawk Chief

In March of 1742, a baby boy was born in a hunting village on the banks of the Ohio River, in what is now the United States. His Mohawk parents called him Thayendanegea, which means "he places two bets." When his father died soon after his birth, his mother returned to her people in the Mohawk valley, taking Thayendanegea and his sister with her. In time, his mother married a Mohawk chief known to the settlers as Brant. Thayendanegea was called "Brant's Joseph," and later Joseph Brant.

His sister Molly married General Sir William Johnson, who was the British superintendent of

Indian affairs. When the Seven Years War between France and England was declared in 1756, Sir William was called to duty. In 1758, teenaged Joseph and other warriors followed him into battle.

In 1760, when his part in the fighting was over, Joseph was taken under the wing of his brother-in-law. Impressed by the young man's abilities, Sir William decided that the boy should receive an education, and when he was 19, Joseph entered Moor's Indian Charity School in Lebanon, Connecticut. During the two years he was there, he learned to read and write English. Joseph became a Christian and acted as an interpreter for an Anglican missionary, since he spoke at least three of the Six Nations languages. Together they translated the Gospel According to St. Mark and the *Book of Common Prayer* into Mohawk.

When he left school, Joseph worked for Sir William. In 1774 Sir William suffered a stroke and died. His title and estates were taken on by his son Sir John Johnson and his duties as superintendent went to his son-in-law Guy Johnson. Joseph became Guy Johnson's secretary. He was appointed inter-preter for the Six Nations languages and paid a yearly salary of about 85 pounds.

But unrest was growing in the American colonies. They wanted independence from Britain. A revolution was just beginning when Joseph Brant asked to be sent to England. He wanted to tell King George III about his concern for the Iroquois peoples and their lands. He and Sir John set sail for London on November 11, 1775.

Joseph was a talented speaker. When he met the king he said, "I bow to no man for I am considered a prince among my own people. But I will gladly shake your hand." The court was very impressed by the way Joseph presented himself, and he was assured that after the war the Iroquois nations would have England's support.

By the time Joseph and Sir John returned in 1776, the fighting had begun. Many of the tribes wanted to stay neutral, but Joseph believed that the key to his people's survival was to remain loyal to England. It was the only way to keep the American colonists from taking over Native lands. He was able to convince the Mohawk, Cayuga, Seneca and Onondaga of the Six Nations to fight alongside the British. Joseph organized a force of about three hundred warriors and a hundred settlers that was called Brant's Volunteers. He was made a captain, but preferred to fight as a war chief. Raiding across the northern frontier, he and his men not only fought for the British Crown, but helped both Native and non-Native Loyalists to escape.

"Every man of us thought by fighting for the King we should ensure a good inheritance for ourselves and our children," he once said. But after the war, in 1783, Britain ignored its Native allies during the peace negotiations. All the land as far west as the Mississippi River was turned over to the Americans. Brant was unable to obtain a land grant for his people from the new American government.

Finally, because of Brant's persistence and leadership, he and the Mohawks were given about 273,000 hectares of land by the British in what is now Ontario. "Six miles deep from either side" of the Grand River, it stretched from the river's source to its mouth. The place where Joseph Brant and his

Mohawk village, Grand River, ca. 1793 (Brant's house is at left)

people crossed became known as "Brant's ford" and eventually as the town of Brantford.

This was a time of great change for Native people. Their way of life – one of hunting and farming using traditional methods – could no longer support them. Brant encouraged them to adopt a new lifestyle. In 1785 a church was built on the reserve. Today is it called Her Majesty's Chapel of the Mohawks. A sawmill and a school were constructed and a schoolmaster was hired. Joseph Brant's decision to sell or lease some of the land to white settlers as a source of income for the community was not popular with everyone. Still, for

Her Majesty's Chapel of the Mohawks, Brantford, Ontario

The Joseph Brant Museum (a replica of Wellington Square) in Burlington, Ontario many years he was a spokesman for the Mohawks, working to bring them and many other tribes together to form a confederacy.

Joseph Brant received a pension from the British government. In 1795, he moved from Grand River and built a house, which he called Wellington Square, near Burlington Bay, Ontario. There he lived in style – he had servants and slaves – with his third wife Catherine and their seven children.

He died in his home on November 24, 1807, and was buried nearby. His remains were moved in 1850 to the graveyard of the Mohawk chapel. In 1886 a bronze statue was unveiled in Brantford to honour Joseph Brant, the Mohawk leader who dedicated his life to the independence of his people.

Statue of Joseph Brant in Brantford, Ontario

Sir John A. Macdonald
Our First Prime Minister

On the Canadian ten-dollar bill, the face of a man stares out. It is that of Sir John Alexander Macdonald.

John began life in Glasgow, Scotland, on January 11, 1815. Five years later he and his family immigrated to Ontario, which was then called Upper Canada. John, his brother, two sisters and his parents settled at Kingston. In time John studied at the Midland District Grammar School. A hard-working student, he loved to read.

There were no law schools in Canada at that time, so when he was 15, John left school and began studying law as an apprentice to George Mackenzie, a Kingston lawyer. By the time he was 17, John Macdonald was the manager of a legal office in Napanee. After Mackenzie died in 1834, John opened his own law office.

In 1837 a group of rebels gathered north of Toronto to protest England's control over Canada. John was a soldier in the militia that confronted the rebels. The next year, by coincidence, he defended several of them at their trials.

Politics began to interest John and he joined the Conservative party. He was a good public speaker whose speeches showed his keen sense of humour. In 1843 he was elected an alderman in Kingston. The next year he won a seat in the Legislative Assembly of the Province of Canada (Canada East and Canada West). He was appointed attorney-general and eventually served as co-premier from 1856 to 1862.

John was a supporter of what was called the Confederation Movement. At that time the British North American Colonies were made up of the Province of Canada, Prince Edward Island, New Brunswick and Nova Scotia. In September of 1864

Delegates at the convention in Charlottetown, P.E.I., September 11, 1864
(Macdonald is sitting on the step at centre)

John attended a conference in Charlottetown, Prince Edward Island. The representatives discussed the idea of joining all the colonies together as one country. Not all were in agreement, but it was a way to make them stronger. The next month they met again, this time in Quebec City, where John spoke convincingly in favour of confederation.

In December of 1866, a third conference began in London, England. With the other delegates, John wrote the British North America Act, a document that set out the way in which the provinces would be united. For his work, he was knighted on June 29, 1867, by Queen Victoria.

Two days later, on July 1, 1867, Canada became a Dominion with four provinces – Ontario, Quebec, New Brunswick and Nova Scotia. These provinces could now more easily trade among themselves. They would also be safer from attack by other countries. Sir John was appointed the first Prime Minister of Canada and won the first federal election in August.

In 1869 Canada took over the western territory that had been controlled by the Hudson's Bay Company. Sir John persuaded other provinces to join the new country. Manitoba became part of Confederation in 1870. British Columbia was promised that a transcontinental railway would be built to connect it to the rest of the country within 10 years, and so it joined in 1871. There were many scandals involved in the building of the railway, though. Because of this, Sir John resigned in 1873, the year Prince Edward Island joined Confederation. But he was re-elected five years later and the building of the Canadian Pacific Railway went on.

Not everyone had wanted a railway. In Manitoba the Métis – people of Native and French blood – saw it as the beginning of the end of their

Sir John and Lady Macdonald stop to admire British Columbia
on their train trip to the Pacific coast in 1886.

traditional lifestyle. They were buffalo hunters, and the trains were bringing settlers to what was once empty prairie. To keep law and order in Canada's west, Sir John had created the North West Mounted Police. Its job was to establish friendly relationships with the Native peoples, so that settlers could arrive in peace.

The Métis had petitioned Ottawa for land of their own. Unsuccessful, they rose up in rebellion, along with other Native peoples. The Northwest Rebellion was crushed and the Métis leader Louis Riel was tried and sentenced to hang. Sir John blocked all attempts to have Riel's sentence changed. On November 16, 1885, nine days after the Canadian Pacific Railway was finished, Riel was executed. His death deepened the division between the French and English in Canada.

Over the years Sir John faced problems in his private life. His first wife died, as did one of their two sons. He and his second wife had a daughter born with brain damage. They named her Mary, but he fondly called her Baboo. She had difficulty controlling her hands, but she learned to use a typewriter and exchanged letters with him. Mary would sometimes attend Parliament to see her father speak.

THE OLD FLAG.
THE OLD POLICY,
THE OLD LEADER.

An 1891 election campaign poster
for Sir John A. Macdonald

At times Sir John turned to drinking, but he remained optimistic about life and was devoted to his daughter. Even when he was criticized, he carried on with his work and kept his sense of humour.

The Right Honourable Sir John A. Macdonald died on June 6, 1891, while still in office. Thousands came to Ottawa to see his coffin lying in state at Parliament. People lined the railway tracks to watch a train take his body back to Kingston where it was laid to rest. He once said, "Let us be English or let us be French . . . and above all let us be Canadians." Sir John A. Macdonald, a Father of Confederation and a true nation builder, had left behind him a Canada that stretched from sea to sea, united by ribbons of steel.

WILLIAM NOTMAN
PHOTOGRAPHER

MONTREAL, OTTAWA, TORONTO.
TO THE QUEEN

COPYRIGHT

Portrait of Sir John A. Macdonald, 1868

Old Guard dinner, 1882, in honour of Sir John A. Macdonald (standing)

Sir Sam Steele
A Man of Action and Duty

Samuel Benfield Steele was born on January 5, 1849, in Medonte Township in Ontario, which was at that time called Canada West. The son of Elmes and Anna Steele, Samuel was first educated at the family home of Purbrook, and then went to a private school in Orillia. As a boy he learned to ride a horse and to hunt. He recalled how he was taught to "make gun powder and ball, using the heavy rifle or fowling piece as soon as we could carry them."

Sam was 11 years old when his mother died. When his father died five years later, he went to live with his older half-brother John. In 1866, 17-year-

old Samuel joined the militia and discovered something about himself – he was meant to be a soldier and to live a life of action and adventure. The next years saw the beginning of a lifelong military career, during which he would be involved in some of the most exciting events of Canada's growth.

In 1870 a force was formed to keep the peace at Red River in Manitoba. Samuel volunteered, joining the 1st Battalion of Rifles. He had been an officer, but this time he chose to serve as a private. "As far as experience went," he would later write, "I . . . learned how to appreciate the trials of other men . . . "

Then, in 1873, Sir John A. Macdonald, the Prime Minister, decided that a policing force was needed to protect Canada's people and interests in

the west. He created the North West Mounted
Police. Sam Steele joined up. He was given the rank
of sergeant-major, and in October he returned to the
west with the first 300 NWMP.

The second stage of the journey was long and
difficult, with shortages of food for the horses and
cattle. Steele kept a journal. On July 19, 1874, he
wrote, "the pattering noise on the tents . . . proved
to be caused by the visitation of locusts, which
afflicted the province of Manitoba so sorely that
year. The air for the height of hundreds of yards was
full of them, their wings shining in the sun, and the
trees, grass, flowers, and in fact everything in sight,
was covered by them."

An entry made on September 27 reads, "Tired
of ducks, geese, prairie chickens and pemmican, the
Métis caught skunks, boiled them in three waters

and then roasted them, thinking them preferable to any other food!"

In 1878 Steele was given his own command at Fort Qu'Appelle. When the Canadian Pacific Railway was being built in the early 1880s, it became his job to settle disputes between the railway builders and the settlers. Respected not only because of his size — he was a large, strong man — he proved again to be hard-working and well-organized.

Inspector Sam Steele and his detachment at Beavermouth, B.C., 1885

During the Northwest Rebellion of the Métis and Native peoples in 1885, Sam led a group of mounted soldiers called Steele's Scouts in pursuit of some of the rebels. He established Fort Steele in 1887 and then went on to Fort Macleod in 1888. It was here that he met his future wife. By 1892 he and his men were policing the entire railway, so Sam moved their headquarters to a new post at Regina, Saskatchewan.

When gold was discovered in the Klondike in 1896, Sam Steele and the NWMP went in to keep order. Within two years he and his men were policing all of the Yukon. He wrote that, "I retired to rest about 2 a.m. or later, rose at six, was out of doors at seven, walked five miles up the Klondike on the ice and back over the mountain, visited every institution under me each day . . ."

In Dawson, as well as keeping the peace, he organized firefighters and

Colonel Sam Steele with his daughter Flora, 1899

made sure the mail was delivered. Anyone arrested was forced to leave or was fined. Some were put to work shovelling snow, washing dishes or — the worst of all — cutting wood. "That wood pile was the talk of the town and kept 50 or more toughs of Dawson busy every day," he wrote.

When the Boer War broke out in South Africa in 1899, Sam Steele volunteered. He was offered the command of Lord Strathcona's Horse, whose job was to scout out the enemy's position, among other tasks. After the war Steele took charge of the police force in South Africa. In 1907 he returned to Canada to write his memoirs, the story of his adventures.

When World War I erupted, Sam Steele again requested active duty. At first his request was denied, since he was 65 years old. He eventually became the commander of the Canadian troops in England, reaching the rank of Major General. On January 1, 1918, he was knighted.

Sir Samuel Benfield Steele died of influenza in England on January 30, 1919. His body was brought back to Canada for burial. There was a general strike going on in Winnipeg on the day of his funeral in June. Riots had been raging, but the strikers and the Mounties called a truce. The strikers bowed their heads as the procession passed by. It was a last sign of respect for Sir Sam Steele – soldier, leader and one of Canada's first peacekeepers.

Pierre
in 1938

Pierre Trudeau

A Leader of Vision

On October 18, 1919, a baby boy was born in Montreal, Quebec. He was christened Joseph Philippe Pierre Ives Elliott Trudeau. Pierre was raised with his brother and sister in a household where both English and French were spoken, since his father Charles was a successful Quebec businessman and his mother Grace was of Scottish descent. This would help mould the way he saw Canada.

He first attended school at the Académie Querbes, where he was sometimes dropped off by the family chauffeur. On his first day in Grade 1, he decided that he was in the wrong grade. At his father's urging, Pierre complained to the principal. He was placed in Grade 2.

Through the years, Pierre continued to be a successful student. He graduated from law school at the University of Montreal and went on to other universities in Canada, the United States, France and England.

After finishing school, Pierre backpacked through eastern Europe and parts of Asia. He applied his talents to a number of careers. In the 1950s he was a political writer for *Cité Libre* in Montreal, and later a professor of law.

But politics called to him. Pierre Trudeau was elected as a Liberal member of Parliament in 1965. Trudeau was not the usual political figure. Floppy hats, capes and a red rose in the buttonhole of his lapel were his trademarks. He liked skiing, white-water canoeing and sliding down banisters. One day he was criticized for what he was wearing in the House of Commons. Instead of a regular tie, he wore a yellow ascot with his button-down shirt. Not bothered in the least, Trudeau said that "people are more interested in ideas than dress."

Within three years Pierre Trudeau became the

Trudeau waves after winning the Liberal leadership convention in 1968 (above), and dances for supporters during the election campaign that follows (right).

The Prime Minister descends from the grandstand to present the 1970 Grey Cup trophy (left).

leader of the Liberal party and Canada's 15th prime minister, taking over from Lester B. Pearson when he retired in early 1968. In June there was an election. Trudeaumania (a word that described his popularity) grew rapidly, and he won.

The next year, Parliament passed an act making English and French the two official languages of Canada. Trudeau declared that English and French Canadians could now choose to live together

41

without giving up their cultures.

Then in 1970 the October Crisis erupted. The FLQ – *Front de Libération de Québec*, or the Quebec Liberation Front – kidnapped the Quebec Labour Minister Pierre Laporte and the British Trade Commissioner James Cross. Trudeau reacted quickly, saying, "We will not negotiate with terrorists." He invoked the War Measures Act, which allowed police to arrest people without a warrant. More than 450 Quebecers were taken into custody. Most of them had committed no crime, and were never charged. Canadian troops were sent out into the streets of Ottawa and Montreal. Although Pierre Laporte was found murdered, James Cross was eventually released.

Prime Minister Trudeau makes a statement about
the release of James Cross (1970).

Pierre and Margaret Trudeau

Justin, "Sacha" and Michel at their father's
office on Parliament Hill (1979).

The next year Pierre Trudeau married 22-year-old Margaret Sinclair. Soon they had three beloved sons – Justin, "Sacha" and Michel.

Trudeau had been prime minister for 11 years when, in 1979, the Conservatives won the federal election and Joe Clark took his place. The Liberals were re-elected 10 months later, and Trudeau was once again prime minister.

Pierre Trudeau was determined to reform the Canadian constitution. In 1981, after much discussion, every province except Quebec agreed that Canada would bring the constitution home from Great Britain. A new bill of rights and freedoms would be added to it.

Prime Minister Trudeau smiles as the Queen signs the Constitution Act on Parliament Hill (1982).

On April 17, 1982, Queen Elizabeth II signed the Constitution Act and proclaimed the new constitution. When that happened, Canada was able to make changes to its laws and government without asking for permission from the Parliament of Great Britain. Canada was truly an independent country.

Pierre Trudeau's years as prime minister saw many firsts. He was the first Canadian prime minister born in the 20th century. In 1972 he appointed the first female Speaker of the Senate, Muriel McQueen Fergusson. He appointed Jeanne Sauvé as Canada's first woman Speaker of the House of Commons in 1980. In 1984 he made her Canada's first female Governor General.

That same year Trudeau retired from politics and returned to practising law. Each workday he walked to and from his Montreal office. It was a quiet, private stage of his life, during which his daughter, Sarah, was born. Then in 1998, the Trudeau family suffered a terrible blow. Michel Trudeau was killed in an avalanche in British Columbia's Kokanee Glacier Park. He was just 23.

Two years later, on September 28, 2000, the Right Honourable Pierre Elliot Trudeau died at home in Montreal. There was an instant and heartfelt response from Canadians across the country. Gone forever was the leader who had spun a pirouette behind the Queen at Buckingham Palace. After lying in state at the Parliament

Trudeau pirouettes behind Queen Elizabeth (1977).

Buildings in Ottawa, he was buried in the family vault in St-Rémi-de-Napierville, Quebec.

Trudeau was many things in his lifetime — a prime minister, an author, a journalist, a lawyer, an outdoorsman and a thinker. He worked to prevent Canada's economy and culture from being overpowered by other countries. He fought hard against Quebec separatism, saying, "Canada will be a strong country when Canadians of all provinces feel at home in all parts of the country, and when they feel that all Canada belongs to them." Pierre Trudeau will remain a leader who fought for peace, a united country, and the rights of every Canadian.